JOHN POWELL, S.J.

UNCONDITIONAL

Love without Limits

 TABOR ®
PUBLISHING

Allen, Texas

Acknowledgments

Excerpt from Viktor E. Frankl, *Man's Search for Meaning*, translated by Ilse Lasch. Copyright © 1959 by Viktor Frankl. Reprinted by permission of Beacon Press.

Specified excerpts from pages 41-42 and 126 from *The Art of Loving* by Erich Fromm. Volume 9 of World Perspective Series, planned and edited by Ruth Nanda Anshen. Copyright © 1956 by Erich Fromm. Reprinted by permission of Harper & Row, Publishers, Inc., and Allen & Unwin Ltd., London.

Robert Frost, "The Road Not Taken," from *The Poetry of Robert Frost*, edited by Edward Connery Latham. Copyright 1916, © 1969 by Holt, Rinehart and Winston. Copyright 1944 by Robert Frost. Reprinted by permission of Holt, Rinehart and Winston, Publishers; the Estate of Robert Frost; Jonathan Cape Ltd., London.

Excerpt from Carl Jung, *Memories, Dreams, Reflections*, recorded and edited by Aniela Jaffe, translated by

Continued on page 124

Photo Credits

Algimantas Kezys, S.J.   8, 12, 17, 51, 62, 72, 100, 104

Jean-Claude Lejeune   iv, 5, 21, 24-25, 29, 39, 42, 46, 54, 59, 66, 80, 86, 93, 96, 113, 120

Cover design: Karen McDonald
Calligraphy: Bob Niles

Tabor Publishing
One DLM Park
Allen, Texas 75002

Library of Congress Catalog Card Number 78-74154

Printed in the United States of America

ISBN 1-55924-282-5

2 3 4 5   93 92 91 90

Contents

A life principle

**Most of all,
let love guide your life.**
Colossians 3:14

Socrates said that the unexamined life is not worth living. Sooner or later we all ask deep within ourselves: What is life for? It is an important and sometimes painful question. But it is a question that must be asked.

When I ask myself this question, I try to direct it to my stomach rather than to my head. My poor head has memorized so many ideal answers, and these rote responses are ready to come tumbling out as soon as someone presses the right button.

The late and great psychologist Abraham Maslow saw us in pursuit of our human goals and needs according to a definite hierarchy: a ladder with many rungs. The lower rungs of the ladder are the fundamental drives for food, shelter, safety from external threats. The middle rungs are the more precisely human set of needs and goals—the "higher order" needs of dignity, belongingness, love. At the summit of Maslow's ladder are the highest human aspirations: independence and excellence. He calls this state "self-actualization." Of course, we never reach the top, but it is precisely this that keeps us going. Maslow was convinced that we function best when we are striving for something we don't have. I think that, for the most part, this is true.

So I ask you to make with me what Dag Hammarskjold once called "the longest journey, the journey inward" to the center of your being, where answers are not memorized but are very much alive.

It is a reluctant journey to which I invite you. Carl Jung, the renowned psychiatrist, once wrote:

> Wherever there is a reaching down into innermost experience, into the nucleus of personality, most people are overcome by fright, and many run away. . . . The risk of inner experience, the adventure of the spirit, is in any case, alien to most human beings.
>
> **Memories, Dreams, Reflections**

I invite you to reflect with me: What is life for?

Perhaps it would be good if each of us were to sit down and to write out a script for our lives-to-come. Try it sometime. You have a blank check. You can fill in all the amounts of success-failure, tears-laughter, long life-short life, agony-ecstasy. You have complete control over pleasure, power, money, fame, relationships. What would you consider the ideal life? What do you really want most?

Or it may help to write out a description of your "perfect day," or a list of the ten activities you enjoy most. When you reflect on what you have written, you may find your deepest needs and longings in clearer perspective. For example, if you find that during your perfect day or in the activities you enjoy most you are alone, perhaps there is some need, buried deep inside you, for solitude or even a desire to avoid relationships.

The question is: What is life for—for you?

To Win a Place in Heaven

I remember a time, many years ago, when I was in Germany trying to master the language of the "natives." I was privileged to serve for a while as a chaplain in a remote Bavarian convent. The dear little Sister who was assigned to care for my room was eighty-four years old. Every time I left my room, even for a moment, she cleaned it. And I don't mean a superficial cleaning. She would wax the floors, polish the furniture, and so forth. On one occasion when I left my room for a short walk, I came back to find "Schwester" on her knees, putting a final sheen on her waxing job. I laughingly teased her:

> *"Schwester, Sie arbeiten zuviel!"* ("Sister, you work too much!")

The dear and devoted little Sister straightened up (still kneeling) and looked at me with a seriousness that bordered on severity. She said:

> *"Der Himmel ist nicht billig!"* ("Heaven isn't cheap, you know!")

***Of course, we never reach the top,
but it is precisely this that keeps us going.***

God bless her. She was no doubt educated to believe, and she believed with all her heart, that life was supposed to be an ordeal, the price of eternal bliss. Heaven must be bought, and it is not cheap. I feel sure that heaven now belongs to that dear soul, who lived so faithfully according to her lights. (In fact, I think that there must be a roped-off section for special souls like "Schwester.") But I can't believe that this kind of joyless purchase of a place in heaven is really the life to which God is calling us. I do not believe that he intends that we should crawl through a dark tunnel on bleeding hands and knees to have a so-called "pie in the sky when we die." God is not a Shylock, demanding his pound of flesh for eternal life. In fact, I believe that, theologically speaking, eternal life has already begun in us because God's life is already in us. We should be celebrating this. We are the branches to Christ's vine (*see* John 15:5).

Do you remember, as I do, the famous *Salve Regina* prayer? It describes a very sad and forlorn version of human life: ". . . to thee do we cry, poor banished children of Eve, to thee do we send up our sighs, mourning and weeping in this valley of tears." I have often thought that if someone really believed this, life would be very bleak. What Jesus said was: "I have come that you might have life, life to the fullest" (John 10:10). "I have told you these things, that my joy may be in you, and your joy may be perfect" (John 15:11).

A Personal Inventory

You and I must open ourselves to the question: What is life for? We should get right down into the fabric of our daily lives. What am I doing? Is my life a series of deadlines . . . meetings . . . clearing my desk . . . answering phones . . . moving from one crisis to the next? Do I look forward to the stretch of life that is ahead of me? To next week? To the coming year? Is mine a hand-to-mouth existence? Is it a matter of "getting by"? When I wake up in the morning, is my first reaction: "Good morning, God!" or "Good God, morning!"? Am I in a survival contest? Do I feel trapped? Am I just hanging on? Am I asking: How much longer can I take this?

Some of us are afraid, as Carl Jung says, to face these questions because of what the answers might imply. We rather anticipate that someone who really doesn't understand will use our answers to tell us that we have to change our lives—to give up our present jobs, to leave our families, to move to a sunnier climate, and so forth. Of course, it may be that you or I should change something in our lives, but I think it is much more realistic and important to change something in ourselves. It may be that the parasites which are eating away inside us, depriving us of the deeper joys and satisfactions of life, should become the object of our attention.

For example, if I am a "compulsive pleaser" of others, living or dying according to the approval I get for my person or my work, then no change of life, job, family, or climate can possibly help me. No matter where I would go or what I would do, the problem would be with me. I would still be asking those torturous questions: Did that look mean that he didn't like me? . . . She didn't smile. I guess she is unhappy with my performance . . . (A thousand et ceteras.)

The same would be true of the "compulsive perfectionist," who can never experience satisfaction because nothing is ever completely perfect. Such a person is, at least internally, a ruthless critic of everything and everyone. (This person, upon entering heaven, will no doubt suggest to God that he spend a few bucks to fix up the place.)

We should comb through our patterns of action and reaction to locate these or similar distortions in our attitudes, and we must then work at revising those attitudes where necessary. But the more universal and more important reality to be investigated is what I would call a "life principle."

The question is: What is life for—for you?

The Meaning of
a Life Principle

A life principle is a generalized, accepted intention of purpose that is applied to specific choices and circumstances. For example, "Good must be done and evil avoided." If this is one of my life principles, whenever I come to a specific choice involving good and evil, my principle directs me to choose that which is good and to avoid that which is evil.

I would like to suggest that everyone has one dominant life principle. It may be difficult to lure it out of the dark, subconscious regions to face examination in the light, but it is there. There is in each of us a set of needs, goals, or values with which we are psychologically preoccupied. There is something, in all the zigs and zags of daily living, which dominates all our other desires. This life principle runs through the fabric of our choices like the dominant theme in a piece of music: it keeps recurring and it is heard in different settings. Of course, only you can answer for yourself, just as only I can answer for myself: What is my life principle?

For example, some people are above and before all else seeking *safety*. They avoid all places where danger might lurk, even if opportunity could be waiting in the same place. They will take no risks, make no gambles. They stay home at night and reveal their deepest selves to no one. It is better to be safe than sorry, they say. The same kind of thumbnail sketch could be made of a person whose primary concern and life principle is *duty, recognition, money, fame, need, success, fun, relationships, approval of others,* or *power.*

Practice Makes a Perfect Habit

Having a life principle is a matter of psychological economy. It diminishes the wear and tear of having to make all decisions from the ground up. For example, if my life principle is *fun,* then whenever I come upon a choice or receive two invitations for the same evening, I simply have to apply my life principle: Where will I have the most fun? My fundamental option or choice is having fun. I have already, consciously or unconsciously, accepted that as a life principle. The specific options or choices are easy. I don't have to go searching through my soul to find out what it is that I am really looking for in life. I already know that. The only uncertainty with which I must deal is: Where will I have the most fun? Having such a life principle, as we said, is a matter of psychological economy.

It is very important to realize that we are creatures of habit. Every time we think a certain

way, seek a certain good, use a given motive, a habit is forming and deepening in us. Like a groove that is being furrowed, each repetition adds a new depth to the habit. (Have you ever tried to break a habit? Then you know what I am trying to say.)

And so it is with a life principle, whatever it be. With each use it becomes a deeper and more permanent habit. And in the twilight of life our habits rule us. They define and dictate our actions and reactions. We will, as the old saying goes, die as we have lived. People who in old age prove quite self-centered and demanding, as well as those who are "mellow" and tolerant, did not become so only in their last years of life. Old cranks have practiced all their lives, just as old saints have likewise practiced all their lives. They just practiced different life principles. What you and I will become in the end will be just more and more of what we are deciding and trying to be right now. There is a fundamental choice, a life principle, which will one day possess us in the marrow of our bones and the blood in our veins. It is a certainty that we will die as we have lived.

"Heaven isn't cheap, you know!"

The Life Principle
of Jesus

In the so-called temptation narratives which are
recorded in Luke 4:1–13, we find Jesus, at the
beginning of his public life, clarifying his own life
principle. More specifically, we find him rejecting
three life principles suggested to him by the devil.
Jesus waited until he was thirty to begin his public
life, because that was the acceptable age for a man
to begin his practice as a rabbi (teacher). At this time,
before beginning what we call his public life, Jesus
was led by the Spirit into the desert.

> Then Jesus, full of the Holy Spirit, left the
> Jordan River, being urged by the Spirit out
> into the barren wastelands of Judea, where
> Satan tempted him for forty days. He ate
> nothing all that time, and was very hungry.
>
> Satan said, "If you are God's Son, tell this
> stone to become a loaf of bread." But Jesus
> replied, "It is written in the Scriptures, 'Other
> things in life are much more important than
> bread!' "
>
> Then Satan took him up and revealed to
> him all the kingdoms of the world in a
> moment of time; and the devil told him, "I
> will give you all these splendid kingdoms and

their glory—for they are mine to give to anyone I wish—if you will only get down on your knees and worship me." Jesus replied, "We must worship God, and him alone. So it is written in the Scriptures."

Then Satan took him to Jerusalem to a high roof of the Temple and said, "If you are the Son of God, jump off! For the Scriptures say that God will send his angels to guard you and to keep you from crashing to the pavement below!" Jesus replied, "The Scriptures also say, 'Don't experiment with God's patience.' " Luke 4:1-12

The first temptation, we might say, was to accept the life principle of *pleasure*. Jesus had fasted, a total fast from all food, and was very hungry. The promise of the devil was the satisfaction of his physical hunger. The reply of Jesus was: "Other things in life are much more important than bread!"

So the devil takes Jesus up to a high place and shows him all the glittering kingdoms of the world and promises him *power* over all these places and peoples. Jesus firmly rejects this life principle: "We must worship God, and him alone." Jesus will give his heart neither to the pursuit of pleasure nor the flattery of power.

So Satan takes Jesus up to the pinnacle of the Temple and urges him to throw himself off. "Let

your Father catch you in the arms of his angels!" the
devil taunts, but Jesus is resolute. He will not
abdicate his personal responsibility for his life. I see
this third temptation precisely in this way. It implies
that we are not really free anyway. It asks us to
accept a kind of determinism that rationalizes an
avoidance of responsibility. Jesus is firm: "Don't
experiment with God's patience."

In this clarification of his own life principle, Jesus
is stating firmly: "I will not live for pleasure! I will
not live for power! I will not surrender responsibility
for my life and my actions!"

Life Principles:
Freud, Adler, Skinner

These same three principles, rejected by Jesus, have
been proposed by three of the great names in the
history of psychology as *the* life principles of all
human beings.

Everyone has one dominant life principle.
It may be difficult to lure it out
of the dark . . . but it is there.

Sigmund Freud (1856–1939) has been traditionally associated with the *pleasure drive* or *pleasure principle*. In the first part of his career he thought that all neuroses were due to sexual repression. Later he realized that there are other personal factors involved, but he continued to use the word *libido* (the Latin word for "desire" or "lust") to describe the instinctual energies and desires that are derived from the so-called *id*. In the Freudian construct, the *id* represents our (animal) drives: vanity, gluttony, lust. It is the source of energy which manifests itself in emotional drives. These impulses are unrefined and primitive, bent only upon immediate gratification. Of course, Freud taught that this basic desire for pleasure had to be moderated. This moderation is done by the *superego* (censor), which means that there is a constant tension in every person between wish and morality. This tension is to be resolved by the ego (the self or the "I"). The ego is a kind of executive part of our psychological makeup, which tries to regulate our desires by adjusting them to reality. The point is that human drives are strongly animalistic—drives for pleasure, for personal gratification. Whether frustrated or moderated, the pleasure principle is the fundamental drive in all humans, according to Freud.

Alfred Adler (1870–1937) was Freud's pupil and disciple until 1911, when he left the "Master" to start his own school of "Individual Psychology," so called because he thought that every human being represented a unique psychological problem. He accused Freud of applying a general formula indiscriminately to all. More specifically, Adler believed Freud's basic error was his universal application of the assumption that frustration of *libido* (the pleasure principle) was always at the heart of every human problem. However, as Adler progressed with his own thought, he fell into the same fallacy of universal application in his formula of compensation-for-inferiority. Adler saw sex and *libido* only as a setting for the *struggle to gain power.* He interpreted all relationships as struggles for power: the child trying to throw off parental authority, a husband and wife each striving for dominance, and so forth. It all begins, according to Adler, with an inferiority complex. This complex is universal, and there is in everyone a desire to compensate for a sense of inferiority. Of course, Adler proposed that the basic desire and struggle for power, as a compensation for inferiority feelings, should be channeled into positive and useful accomplishments. But this was his assumption and interpretation: The basic drive in people is for power and accomplishment.

B. F. Skinner is a contemporary psychologist who proposes that it is neither pleasure nor the pursuit of power that writes the script for human life. He contends that we are the irreversible result of our conditioning or programming. This logically invites us to *avoidance of responsibility* for our lives. "Operant conditioning" is based on the assumption that if we find a certain type of behavior rewarding, we tend to repeat it. If it produces negative results, we avoid it and try something else. In his book *Beyond Human Freedom and Dignity,* Skinner attempts to refute the theory that we can choose our own life principle. According to him, it is not our lot to choose anything. His is a theory of behaviorism that amounts to determinism. If one were to accept this, it would mean abdication of all personal responsibility for one's life and actions. The attitude of such a person would be to wait and see what life holds in store, to see how things turn out. One would regard his or her life story as a phonograph record, already imprinted, complete in all details, as the result of programming in infancy. During one's lifetime the phonograph record is in the process of spinning out. The process is automatic. The story cannot be changed. We are predetermined. No adult really exercises either freedom or responsibility. Or so says Skinner.

What you and I will become in the end will be just more and more of what we are deciding and trying to be right now.

Inroads into My Own Life

Of course, there is *some* truth in what each of these three men has written. (It is hard to be totally wrong.) We have only to consult our own personal experience to know that there is in us a drive toward pleasure and toward power. We are likewise aware that certain reactions, prejudices, phobias, and so forth have been programmed into us. We have to acknowledge that our freedom has been limited to some extent by the early experiences of our lives.

Still each of us has a leverage of freedom, an ability to choose, to clarify our own values, and to act on chosen motives. It is good for us to look back over the choices of the past: Which of the proposed life principles has tended to dominate my life? Has the story of my life been a pursuit of *pleasure?* Or have I been competitive, ambitious, intoxicated by the raw liquor of *power?* Perhaps neither has been the driving force in my life. It may be that there has been no driving force in my life. Perhaps I have let life roll over me. I have decided by not deciding. It may be that I have accepted the *avoidance-of-responsibility* life principle, which has led me to abdicate responsibility for the direction and outcome of my life. (There is a consensus, by the way, that most people today have given up all serious hope that they can determine or even change their lives.)

Gospel Characters:
Life Principles Illustrated

In the Gospels we find individuals who seem to be personifications of these three life principles. Herod seems to be dominated by the pleasure principle. I think that Herod was drunk when Jesus was brought before him for judgment.

> Now when Herod saw Jesus, he was very happy. He had wanted for a long time to see Jesus since he had heard so much about him. He was hoping to see some exhibition of his magical powers. He asked Jesus a string of questions, but Jesus didn't answer any of them. Now the chief priests and the Scribes were standing around and were angrily accusing him. Finally, Herod, joined by his soldiers, began to treat Jesus with a mocking contempt. They finally clothed him with a bright robe and sent him back to Pilate.
>
> **Luke 23:8-11**

"I will not live for pleasure!
I will not live for power!
I will not surrender responsibility
for my life and my actions!"

My suspicion that Herod was drunk comes not only from secular history's portrayal of him as a weak, pleasure-bent man, but is also based on the fact that Jesus would not speak to him. He would not speak to him because it would have done no good. This man, who had been educated at the imperial court of Rome, was surrounded by his own "nobility," called the Herodians. They supported him in all his whims, including his divorce from his wife in order to take his half-brother's wife, who was his own niece, Herodias. When John the Baptist fearlessly denounced this marriage as sinful, Herod imprisoned him. He seems to have been completely controlled by Herodias, who persuaded her daughter, Salome, to ask for the head of John the Baptist. I think that Herod was drunk on this occasion, too, when he expressed such great pleasure with Salome's dancing that he promised her anything . . . up to half of his kingdom.

When Jesus came before Herod, I think that Herod regarded him only as some kind of magician, who would do a few sleight of hand tricks for the entertainment of his court. When Jesus met his intoxicated demands with silence, Herod in effect pronounced this sentence: "I am ready to pronounce judgment. This man is crazy! Here I have the power over his life and he just stands there, a silent fool. He is crazy, insane. Take him back to Pilate, clothed in the robe of a fool."

Poor Herod had a ring in his nose. It was the ring of pleasure. It was his life principle, the underlying motive that ruled all his choices and shaped his entire life. He was owned by the pursuit of pleasure.

On the other hand, I see Pontius Pilate as a man whose life was ruled by the desire for power. About five to ten years before he sentenced Jesus to die, he was appointed by Rome to rule Judea, Samaria, and Idumea. Like many power-thirsty people, Pilate was a cruel man. He flaunted the religious sensibilities of the Jews, whom he was sent to rule, by erecting graven images of the emperor. He confiscated money from their Temple treasury to finance an aqueduct. He ruthlessly slaughtered a group of worshiping Galileans. He minted coins bearing the image of offensive pagan religious symbols. At one time Pilate was ordered back to Rome to stand trial for cruelty and oppression. A letter from Herod Agrippa I to Caligula describes him as "inflexible, merciless, and corrupt." He was often accused of holding executions without trial. An uncertain tradition, reported by the historian Eusebius, has it that he killed himself on orders from Caligula, shortly after he sentenced Jesus to die.

Pilate's life clearly reveals that his life principle was power. It is easy to imagine him as he uses his barbarian soldiers to inflict terrible cruelties in order to establish his privilege of power. He knows that if he succeeds in his present commission, he will get a higher, more prestigious post. It is all he really cares about.

So when Jesus is brought before him, the charge for which Jesus was convicted in the Sanhedrin— that he claimed to be the Messiah and the Son of God—is not even mentioned. It would have meant nothing to Pilate, who was a polytheist. He could have shrugged that off. With all the gods that Rome worshiped, divinity was not a serious concern for him. And so the charge before Pilate was tailored for one whose only concern was power: "He claims to be a king!" Ah! This would indeed impress poor Pontius Pilate. If word got back to Rome that some simple Jew claimed to be a king and Pilate did not crush him, his political career would be over. He would lose his power. So Pilate offers to interview Jesus.

In effect he says to him: "You're not really a king, are you? Is that what they said out there? You don't look like a king to me." Jesus responds: "I am truly a king, but my kingdom is not of this world. I am not

*It may be that there has been
no driving force in my life.*

competing with you. But I am a king. This is why I
was born and why I have come into this world. This
is the truth, and those who really want the truth
will hear my voice." (*See* John 18:33-37.)

Then Pilate asks his famous question: "What is
truth?" What does it matter if you have truth on
your side? It is power that counts. Pilate can think
only in terms of power: he cannot recognize any other
value.

But something happens to Pilate in that interview with Jesus. He does everything he can to avoid
pronouncing the sentence of crucifixion. He returns
to the porch of his palace and raises his hands for
silence: "I find him not guilty!" he bellows. When the
demand is chanted again and again, "Crucify that
Galilean!" Pilate becomes aware that Jesus is a
Galilean. He recalls that Herod has power to preside
over cases involving Galileans. So he tries the escape
of sending Jesus off to Herod. When Jesus is returned
to him, Pilate tries a second subterfuge. In one of
history's classic *non sequiturs,* he says: "I find him
not guilty. Therefore, I will chastise him and release
him." It proves futile.

Another avenue of escape occurs to Pilate: the
custom of the Procurator of Rome to release a
prisoner at festival time. He gives the crowd a choice
between a notorious criminal, Barabbas, or Jesus.
They choose Barabbas. When Pilate's wife, Claudia,

sends a message to him at this point, saying that she has had a bad dream and warning him not to yield to the demands of the mob, Pilate is irritated. He is trying with all his strength to get out of this predicament. He offers again to have Jesus chastised before release, but the mob's clamoring for his death is unyielding.

Pilate makes a last attempt to escape the inevitable. "Do you want to see blood? I will show you blood!" He orders Jesus to be scourged. When Jesus is brought before the crowd, a red mask of agony, Pilate moans: "Do you see this? What you see here is a man. Look at the man." Once more he pronounces: "Take him yourselves and crucify him. I find him not guilty."

But the mob cries: "If you release this man, you are no friend of Caesar; for everyone who makes himself a king sets himself against Caesar!" (John 19:12).

"Shall I crucify your king?"

"We have no king but Caesar."

So Pilate breaks a small, dry twig in the face of Jesus and pronounces the sentence: *"Ibis ad crucem!"* ("You will go to the cross!") The mob senses his weakness. They have Pilate where he hurts. His power is at stake. Power, power, power.

In a last ironic gesture, he calls for a boy with a bowl of water: "I wash my hands of the blood of this man." But Pilate's lust for power had owned him and had led him into places he did not want to go. He had built a life on the pursuit of power, and in the end it destroyed him.

The Gospel personality who seems to suggest, if not personify, the avoidance-of-responsibility life principle is the invalid at the Bethesda pool.

Inside the city, near the Sheep Gate, was Bethesda Pool, with five covered platforms or porches surrounding it. Crowds of sick folks—lame, blind, or with paralyzed limbs— lay on the platforms (waiting for a certain movement of the water, for an angel of the Lord came from time to time and disturbed the water, and the first person to step down into it afterwards was healed). One of the men lying there had been sick for thirty-eight years. When Jesus saw him and knew how long he had been ill, he asked him, "Would you like to get well?"

"I can't," the sick man said, "for I have no one to help me into the pool at the movement of the water. . . ." Jesus told him, "Stand up, roll up your sleeping mat and go on home!" Instantly, the man was healed!

John 5:2–9

Actually we know very little about this poor man, and perhaps our use of him as an example is unfair. However, he seems to have been assigning his plight to the unwillingness of others to help him. He also seems to have lost hope. Like many people who do not want to assume responsibility for their lives, he talks only about what others are not doing for him. Apparently he has not given much thought to how he might help himself. He is so absorbed in the limitations of his condition that he does not explore the creative possibilities of the situation.

And so Jesus asks the man a question that moves him to probe his own inner attitudes: "Would you really like to get well?" Some people, as we know, make a vocation of being sick, either physically or emotionally. It is the easiest, if not the only, way for them to relate to others: by being needy. Sometimes sickness provides an excuse for not trying. The American Academy of Psychosomatic Medicine has theorized that 92 percent of all physical illness is psychologically induced. It would seem that many people, at least subconsciously, prefer to be sick— even to the point of resisting obvious means to health—simply because they have given up on their capacity to cope with life. They cannot accept the challenges of life so they retreat into some physically or emotionally disabling condition. Illness is passive. Involvement is active. They choose passivity rather than activity in life.

There are many other rationalizations, besides the excuse of sickness, which are used to justify the avoidance-of-responsibility life principle. Sometimes we let our fears or our self-inflicted judgments of inferiority shield us from taking the risks and facing the challenges of a full life. We substitute "I can't" for "I won't even try." I remember a former student of mine explaining to me why he was withdrawing from all his classes just before final exams. "It is easier not to have tried than to have tried and failed. If you don't try, you can always console yourself by saying: 'I probably could have done it.' If you try and fail, you don't even have that dubious consolation."

When one sets out to look for avenues of escape, the possibilities are infinite. "This is the way I am!" Some people blame their life condition on their genes. Others claim that their level of education is responsible for their life's outcome. Still others assign their fixed state to ethnic background or lack of connections. A large group of people "blame it on the stars." This tendency to use astrology as a way out of personal responsibility is an old one: a tried and true rationalization.

"Men at some time are masters of their fate.
The fault, Dear Brutus, is not in our stars,
But in ourselves. . . ."
Julius Caesar (I, ii, 134)

Not to Judge
But to Understand

The point is not to set oneself on the throne of judgment, or to pity from a privileged position those who have been duped by the fountains of pleasure or lured into the palaces of power. Nor can we diagnose with disdain those who seem to have given up and accepted life as a passive spectator sport. The point is, rather, that to some extent all three of these life principles have made inroads and left an imprint on our own life-styles.

So you and I must look into ourselves at the deepest level, the point at which few people, if any, are ever permitted to know us. What do we *really* want from life? What do we *really* think would make us happy? You and I are now practicing a life principle, which may not be obvious from a surface view. Someday it will amount to a life wager. In the end everyone gambles his or her life on something, or someone, as the way to happiness.

The Christian
Life Principle

In the Gospel narrative of the final Passover Feast (the Last Supper), Jesus dramatizes his own life principle and lays before the Apostles and all of us the condition of our own Christian discipleship. Almost immediately after Jesus gives his disciples the bread of his Body and the cup of his Blood, a dispute arises over "which one in their group should be considered the greatest" (Luke 22:24). After three years of tutelage under the greatest of all spiritual directors, the disciples still labor under their old delusions. They are petty, competitive, self-centered.

So in the last hours of his life, Jesus tries to remind them of his central message. He washes their feet. According to Jewish custom, if the host of a dinner was honored by the presence of his guests, he would wash their feet. If, on the contrary, the guests considered themselves honored by the invitation, the host did not wash their feet, presumably indicating his higher social status. You will recall that when Jesus ate with Simon the Pharisee (Luke 7:36–50), Simon did not extend this courtesy.

During the Last Supper or Passover Meal, Jesus

. . . got up from the supper table, took off his robe, wrapped a towel around his loins (as a servant would do). He poured water into a basin and began to wash the feet of his disciples and to dry them with the towel he had around him.

When he came to Simon Peter, Peter said to him: "Lord, are you really going to wash my feet?" Jesus explained, "You may not understand this now, but someday you will understand."

"No!" Peter protested, "you will never wash my feet."

Jesus replied: "If you don't let me wash your feet, you cannot be my partner!"

Simon Peter then exclaimed: "If that is the case, then wash my hands and head, too, not just my feet."

John 13:4-9

During his three years with the Twelve—spending most of the time alone with them, teaching and preparing them for their mission—the central message of Jesus was the kingdom of God. Much of the Gospel narrative concerns the preaching and parables of the kingdom. If this kingdom could be briefly defined, it would certainly imply two things.

First, the kingdom is an invitation from God. It is an invitation to all humankind to come to God in an intimate relationship of love. More vividly, we might imagine God, smiling at us with a warm look of love, stretching forth his arms to embrace us: "Come to me. I will be your God. You will be my People, the children of my heart!" It should be noted that this call or invitation is not extended to us merely as individuals. In the kingdom of God we are never less than individuals, but we are never merely individuals. We are the Body of Christ. We are called to come to God's embrace of love as brothers and sisters in the Lord. The French poet Charles Peguy wrote: "Do not try to go to God alone. If you do, he will certainly ask you the embarrassing question: 'Where are your brothers and sisters?' " In other words, the invitation to the kingdom is extended to us together. I can say "yes" to God only if I say "yes" to you, my brothers and my sisters. It is one and the same "yes" which embraces my God and my human family, all in the same act of love.

Second, on our part, the kingdom of God implies a free response of love. "In the head of the book it is written of me that to do your will is all my delight. Behold I come . . . running!" When we pray in the Lord's Prayer "Thy kingdom come!" we are praying that all of us will say the big "yes" (and all the little "yeses" which will be inside it) to one another and to our Father.

I can say "yes" to God only if I say "yes" to you, my brothers and sisters.

It was this, I feel sure, that Jesus wanted so much to make clear to Peter and the disciples. In all his days with them, but especially at the Last Supper, in his last moments with them, he wanted to underline the truth: My kingdom is a kingdom of love! It is not a place where power rules or people compete. It is not a playground of pleasure or a haven for those who have no heart to try. The solemn and solitary requirement for entrance into the kingdom of God is the choice of love as a life principle. There is only one badge of identification: "By this shall all men know that you are my disciples, that you love one another as I have loved you" (John 13:35).

"If you cannot accept this," Jesus was saying to Peter, "you cannot be my partner. The only power in my kingdom is the power of love!" In the wake of their silly squabbling over who was the most important, Jesus washed their feet and left them with a rather solemn reminder:

> "In this world, kings lord it over their subjects, and those in authority insist that they be called their country's 'benefactor.' Don't let it ever be this way with you. On the contrary, the highest among you must bear himself as though he were the youngest, and the chief among you must act like a servant. Who is greater: the one who sits at table or the servants who wait on him? Surely the one

who sits at table. Yet here I am—I am your servant!" Luke 22:25-27

Jesus wants to know if the lesson has come through. He apparently found in the Apostles the same lack of understanding that I so often find in myself. In Mark's Gospel, Jesus asks the Apostles seventeen times (I once counted them!): "Are you still without understanding?" John writes:

After washing their feet he put on his robe again and sat down with them. Then he asked: "Do you know what I was just doing? You call me 'Master' and 'Lord' and you do well to say this because it is true. And since I, the Lord and Teacher, have washed your feet, you ought to do the same for one another. I have given you an example to follow: do as I have done to you. . . . If you keep this in mind and put it into practice you will be very happy." John 13:12-17

I must ask myself the same question again and again: Do I really understand? Do I really believe that Jesus calls me to accept as my own the life principle of love? Do I really understand that such a commitment is the only way to true and abiding happiness? These are the questions whose answers lie deep inside me. I must at least attempt a search of those deepest parts. My whole life is at stake.

C H A P T E R T W O

The contemporary crisis of love

The crisis of our time
As we are beginning
Slowly and painfully to perceive
Is a crisis not of the hands
But of the hearts.
ARCHIBALD MACLEISH

The English author Gilbert Keith Chesterton once said that there is a double problem with proclaiming the Gospel as the "Good News." First, he suggested, it is not really "news" to many people who have heard it repeated and repeated. Second, it does not sound like "good" news to most people.

Something in me eagerly agrees. To my ears a lot of religious exhortation seems to be aimed about two or three miles above where most people really live. The level of the ideal offered is so clearly beyond reach that all we are left with is inevitable failure and the consequent guilt feelings. Of course, I am not suggesting a massive compromise of our ascetical and moral principles. Such a "cave-in" would be even worse.

The question at hand is this: Is loving really the way to human fulfillment? If I choose love as my personal life principle, will I find satisfaction and true gratification? Are all the Gospel paradoxes about love really valid in the laboratory of life? If I seek myself and my own happiness, is it certain that I will lose both? Does the seed really have to fall into the ground and die before there can be a full and happy life? Is the Gospel beatitude of unselfish and unconditional love really the path to true human joy? These are indeed hard and practical questions—questions which are today the subject of considerable debate.

In fact, I would say that this is the major crisis facing contemporary society. Is a life of love, which involves a permanent and unconditional commitment to the happiness of another, really the way to personal satisfaction and human fulfillment? Or must one rather stay free and unencumbered from all such relationships in order to experience the pleasure, the power, and the variety of sensations which life can offer? Is personal satisfaction and gratification the most fulfilling life goal, or is the deepest meaning in life to be found only in a committed and permanent relationship of love? Should we lay our lives and our persons on the line, or is it better never to say "forever"?

The Denial of Love

Love as the life principle of a meaningful existence has not been accorded the status of a beatitude by contemporary society. In fact, there is a library of recent literature challenging the life principle of love. In the life-styles chosen by many people today, and in the motives they offer for their life-styles, there is a persistent and ruthless questioning of the reality— the very *possibility*—of true, permanent human love. Books pour off the presses—many of them high on best-seller charts—proposing trendy techniques to get the most pleasure and personal satisfaction out of life. The suggested basic mind-set and only pertinent question is: *What's in it for me?*

As a result of this philosophy, many people have taken to reevaluating the investment of their lives. They have measured their life experience according to the recommended criterion: What have I gotten out of life for myself? An alarming number of these people have fallen into a regret-filled despondency as they look at their lives, their jobs, their marriages, and their families. They feel that they have been somehow defrauded, cheated of an exhilarating happiness that could have been theirs. "You only go around once. You have to grab all you can . . . for yourself." They look at what they have grabbed and it is not enough. They are haunted by the fear that they have missed all the tingling satisfactions that could have been theirs. They are sad and wonder where they went wrong. The depressing words repeat themselves slowly and sadly: Is this all there is?

Opportunistic authors have come running with reams of advice and pages of instructions · on self-satisfaction and self-fulfillment. "I will turn these stones to bread. . . . I will give you these cities to rule. . . . I will free you from the struggles of

To my ears a lot of religious exhortation seems to be aimed about two or three miles above where most people really live.

personal responsibility and commitments!" These authors have given detailed instructions on taking care of Number One (me, me, me!), on getting power and keeping it, on winning by the intimidation of others. They have extolled the virtues of selfishness. They have portrayed life as a cutthroat competition and warned that "nice guys finish last!" They have deluged an already sex-drenched generation with the "how to" books, guaranteed to produce increased erotic pleasure. Sexploitation.

These authors have relegated love, marriage, and family to the oblivion of "old-fashioned" ideas. The "in thing" now is creative divorce: how to make the death of a deep relationship the birth of something bright and beautiful. One group actually wrote a ritual to "celebrate" divorce among its members. The authors have encouraged us to shift gears, to pull up all the old roots in order to develop exciting new selves! They have urged us to focus all our attention on ourselves, to be our own best friends now and forever.

Underlying all these suggestions is the belief that human fulfillment is found by the direct pursuit of one's own happiness. To do this, one must be free—free from once-made promises, free from responsibilities and love commitments, free from all the claims others make upon one's life and one's love. This has led many to see their spouses and families as obstacles to their personal fulfillment.

At best these books are dehumanizing; at worst they are positively cruel. In either case they are part of a vast societal rationalization of the self-centered existence. They lie at the farthest point on the spectrum from the commitment of unconditional love. The assumption of this self-fulfillment cult seems to be that to give your word of commitment and your promise of faithfulness to another is really to surrender your own individuality and personal identity.

To me it is obvious that this is simply not true—that the very opposite is true. Unless you give your word and your promise of fidelity to another, there can be no real trust and consequently no authentic relationship or secure framework in which two people can grow.

The Cult of Experience
vs.
Unconditional Commitment

Of course, all of us should at times take inventory of our personal growth and sense of fulfillment. The question "Am I really enjoying my life?" can and very likely will reveal valuable information and put me in touch with unrealized parts of myself. If we find inside us some painful voids, we should reassess our attitudes and perhaps redirect some of our energies. But this is not the issue of contention.

The heart of the matter and the crux of the problem is this: Do we get fulfilled by trying to have all the experiences we can? Is it true that the more experiences a person has, the more developed and fulfilled he or she will be as a person? Or is the contrary true, that a person is fulfilled by making a commitment and then choosing experiences according to whether they honor, promote, and reaffirm the commitment?

Trying to choose all available experiences is like trying to mix oil and water: they just don't blend. The result is confusing, fragmenting, and disintegrating to the human person. For a fulfilling life, we must conceive reality as somehow ordered and meaningful. This implies a value structure, priorities. It is in the light of these values and priorities that we must evaluate experiences. I would like to quote from my own book on religious faith, *A Reason to Live, A Reason to Die:*

The depressing words repeat themselves
slowly and sadly: Is this all there is?

To try to open himself to all possible experiences can only result in an interior chaos; it would break him apart. If a man decides to be a true husband and father, to be loyal and faithful to his marriage commitment, the experience of having a mistress or visiting prostitutes will make his heart and soul a divided city. If a person is determined to grow through contact with reality, which is the only way to grow, the experience of drunkenness or hallucinogenic narcotics will be very crippling to his personal growth.

Becoming a person, therefore, involves the sacrifice of some experiences in order to experience more deeply the values which are connected with and which promote one's own destiny. Having decided what we want to be and want to do, we must exercise some selection in the experiences we seek, choosing those which are conducive to our goals and refusing those which could only detour us.

Making a commitment to permanent, unconditional love will mean for me that certain experiences, which might otherwise have been mine, are now impossible for me. The man who chooses one woman for his wife and life partner by his very choice has eliminated all other women as possible wives and life partners. It is this very elimination that frightens us on the brink of commitment. Every commitment is like every moment in life: there is a birth and a death in every moment. Something is and something else can never be again. There is a choice and a surrender, a "yes" and a "no." To love is indeed costly. To love unconditionally is a life wager. In love we put ourselves on the line and there is no going back. It is at this brink that so many seem to collapse. Within arms' reach of greatness, they faint at the thought of never returning. It is the less traveled road.

The Road Not Taken

Two roads diverged in a yellow wood,
And sorry I could not travel both
And be one traveler, long I stood
And looked down one as far as I could
To where it bent in the undergrowth;

Then took the other, as just as fair,
And having perhaps the better claim,
Because it was grassy and wanted wear;
Though as for that, the passing there
Had worn them really about the same,

And both that morning equally lay
In leaves no step had trodden black.
Oh, I kept the first for another day!
Yet knowing how way leads on to way,
I doubted if I should ever come back.

> I shall be telling this with a sigh
> Somewhere ages and ages hence:
> Two roads diverged in a wood, and I—
> I took the one less traveled by,
> And that has made all the difference.
>
> **ROBERT FROST**

The cult of experience urges us to grab all we can while passing through this world. Besides being internally confusing, such a program is a practical impossibility. It can leave us so fragmented that we might never be able to put our pieces back together again. It will certainly leave us with broken dreams and shattered hopes. If we listen to the preachers and propagandists of this cult, we will resemble the person who wants it all so badly that, in the end, everything is lost. I am reminded of the graphic description of such a person, given in *The Bell Jar* by Sylvia Plath:

> I felt like a racehorse in a world without racetracks or a champion college footballer

Without fidelity there cannot be
an authentic relationship.

suddenly confronted by Wall Street and a business suit, his days of glory shrunk to a little gold cup on his mantel with a date engraved on it like the date on a tombstone.

I saw my life branching out before me like the green fig tree in the story.

From the tip of every branch, like a fat purple fig, a wonderful future beckoned and winked. One fig was a husband and a happy home and children, and another fig was a famous poet, and another fig was a brilliant professor, and another fig was Ee Gee, the amazing editor, and another fig was Europe and Africa and South America, and another fig was Constantine and Socrates and Attila and a pack of other lovers with queer names and offbeat professions, and another fig was an Olympic lady crew champion, and beyond and above these figs were many more figs I couldn't quite make out.

I saw myself sitting in the crotch of this fig tree, starving to death, just because I couldn't make up my mind which of the figs I would choose. I wanted each and every one of them, but choosing one meant losing all the rest, and, as I sat there, unable to decide, the figs began to wrinkle and go black, and, one by one, they plopped to the ground at my feet.

comprise a relatively scant measure of what is commonly called fun and enjoyment. Among those who hold an examined view of the subject, few would deny that a fair share of the goodness of life befell to such persons as Abraham Lincoln, Ghandi, Louis Pasteur, Albert Schweitzer, Dorothea Dix, Dietrich Bonhoeffer, Pope John XXIII, Martin Buber, and Martin Luther King. Hardly anyone, however, would say that these persons' lives were marked by lots of fun. Such contamination of the notion of the good life with that of a good time obscures and distorts the issue.

On Being Human

"Doing My Thing" vs. I-Thou

The tension between self-fulfillment directly sought and self-fulfillment as a by-product of loving is, in my judgment, the greatest crisis facing our society today.

There are two poetic expressions which do not precisely define these opposing positions, but seem to reflect something of their diverse spirits. The first is the familiar "Gestalt Prayer" of Fritz Perls.

I do my thing, and you do your thing.
I am not in this world to live up to your
  expectations,
And you are not in this world to live up
  to mine.
You are you and I am I;
If by chance we find each other,
  it's beautiful.
If not, it can't be helped.

FRITZ PERLS

These lines express very forcibly the human need for independence and self-expression. I must have my own thoughts and feelings and I must assert my right to express them freely. I must make my own choices and be able to live by them. No doubt these were the practical good purposes in the mind of Fritz Perls. I feel sure that he wanted his lines to expose the clinging dependency and jealous possessiveness which are, in fact, counterfeits of true love.

But the waters of pleasure . . .
are always bright on the surface but,
sadly, only one inch deep. We always
come up with sand in our mouths.

At the same time his verse opens itself to serious criticism. In itself and without qualification it sounds like a creed of "subjectivism" which waves the banner-slogan: "Do your own thing!" This kind of subjectivism ignores the fact that we are interrelated and interdependent social beings. I cannot do my thing without somehow affecting you. I cannot light up my big, fat cigar if it will make you sick.

But more profoundly, this subjectivism ignores one of the deepest truths of human existence: For a person to be is to-be-with-others. Human life and human fulfillment are essentially relational. In other words, the Perls credo reflects the human need for independence, but ignores the need for true and deep relationships. Perls prescinds from the warmth, the caring, the empathy and commitment which are so essential to loving, which is in turn so essential to the process of becoming a person.

The supplement, offered by psychologist Walter Tubbs, speaks for itself. It redresses the imbalance in the thought of Perls, giving a fuller view of the human condition. True human fulfillment is found only in relationships of love: "The truth begins with two."

Beyond Perls

If I just do my thing and you do yours,
We stand in danger of losing each other
And ourselves.

I am not in this world to live up to your
   expectations;
But I am in this world to confirm you
As a unique human being.
And to be confirmed by you.

We are fully ourselves only in relation
   to each other;
The I detached from a Thou
Disintegrates.

I do not find you by chance;
I find you by an active life
Of reaching out.

Rather than passively letting things
   happen to me,
I can act intentionally to make them
   happen.

I must begin with myself, true;
But I must not end with myself:
The truth begins with two.

WALTER TUBBS

CHAPTER THREE

The meaning of love

"*It is only with the heart that one can see rightly; what is essential is invisible to the eye.*"

ANTOINE DE SAINT-EXUPÉRY,
The Little Prince

I would like to review briefly at this point some things that I have treated in greater detail in another book, *The Secret of Staying in Love*. Love should be generally supported by favorable feelings, but it is not itself a feeling. If it were a feeling, love would be a very fickle reality and those who construed it to be a feeling would be very fickle people. Rather love is a *decision* and *commitment*. My Christian vocation is to love all people. This means that I must try to do for each person with whom I interact whatever I can to promote that person's true growth and happiness. However, I cannot enter into an actual and ongoing love relationship with everyone. I must therefore decide—and it should be a careful choice— to whom and at what level of commitment I wish to offer my love.

Having made such a decision, on the presumption that my offer of love has been accepted and reciprocated, I am now by my own free choice committed to the happiness, security, and well-being of the person I love. I will do everything I can to help that person build whatever dreams he or she has. It is this commitment which I make when I offer my love. When I question myself about the place love has in my life, I must therefore ask if there is any person in my life whose growth and happiness is as real or more real to me than my own. If so, love has truly entered my life.

soil in which love can possibly grow. "We're gonna make it together!"

Erich Fromm writes of the so-called conditional love:

> Unconditional love corresponds to one of the deepest longings, not only of the child, but of every human being; on the other hand, to be loved because of one's merit, because one deserves it, always leaves doubt; maybe I did not please the person whom I want to love me, maybe this, or that—there is always a fear that love could disappear. Furthermore, "deserved" love easily leaves a bitter feeling that one is not loved for oneself, that one is loved *only* because one pleases, that one is, in the last analysis, not loved at all but used.
>
> *The Art of Loving*

The Message of Unconditional Love

The essential message of unconditional love is one of liberation: You can be whoever you are, express all your thoughts and feelings with absolute confidence. You do not have to be fearful that love will be taken away. You will not be punished for your openness or honesty. There is no admission price to

my love, no rental fees or installment payments to be made. There may be days when disagreements and disturbing emotions may come between us. There may be times when psychological or physical miles may lie between us. But I have given you the word of my commitment. I have set my life on a course. I will not go back on my word to you. So feel free to be yourself, to tell me of your negative and positive reactions, of your warm and cold feelings. I cannot always predict my reactions or guarantee my strength, but one thing I do know and I do want you to know: I will not reject you! I am committed to your growth and happiness. I will always love you.

Unconditional Love and Personal Growth

There is nothing else that can expand the human soul, actualize the human potential for growth, or bring a person into the full possession of life more than a love which is unconditional. We have labored for so long under the delusion that corrections, criticism, and punishments stimulate a person to

"We're gonna make it together!"

grow. We have rationalized the taking out of our own unhappiness and incompleteness in many destructive ways. For example, recent surveys revealed that 80 percent of the inmates in this country's prisons were brutalized as children. Only recently have the behavioral sciences reached the point of enlightenment to show us that unconditional love is the only soil in which the seed of a human person can grow.

Of course, free will is a factor in every human life. Everyone must say his or her "yes" to growth and integrity. But there are prerequisites. And one of these is that someone must empower me to believe in myself and to be myself. Only someone who loves me unconditionally can do this.

When we think of conditional love, we immediately think of manipulative parents. We think of parents giving their children affection and affirmation only when the conditions are met: when the children get good grades, obey the rules, make their parents proud, and so forth. We think of husbands and wives who do the same things to each other. The games people play. The hugs and kisses when the house is clean, in return for punctuality or a special dinner. The pan-scales always show through conditional love: it is an exchange, a reciprocal bargain, not a free gift. We often overlook a more subtle form of conditional love: the "operant conditioning" of which B. F. Skinner writes. We give to those whom we wish to manipulate appropriate rewards for being what we want them to be. We assign to them an identity of our choosing. We paint them into a small corner of life, allowing them to be only what we have decided they should be. Unconditional love is liberating. It frees the loved one to be authentic and real. Operant conditioning leaves the loved one only the course of conformity.

The Story of Katie

A few years ago a woman named Margaret Stern Mattisson shared with us a shattering episode from her own life. She called her story, published in *Reader's Digest,* "Love Is Not Enough." The summary line beneath the title read: "Our daughter was bright, loving, popular, successful—'perfect,' we felt, in every way. And then one awful night she tried to end her life."

Margaret Mattisson very courageously told the story of her child, Katie, the ideal daughter. She told of the unexpected phone call which came to the church hall during the production of a musical in which Margaret Mattisson was playing a part. It was Katie gasping, struggling: "Mother, come home. . . . I've taken sleeping . . . sleeping . . . sleep . . ." Then the crash of the phone and Katie to the floor, the frantic phone calls to neighbors, the ambulance siren, the white hospital sheets, and the still unconscious form of Katie, the perfect daughter, who tried to end her life. The unspoken question that ached in her mother and father at her bedside was: Why? Fortunately Katie did revive. But when she sat up in the first glimmerings of consciousness, it was anger, not pathos, that spewed from her: an astonishing array of angry, vulgar epithets. Katie had never, never sworn before. These were words it was supposed she did not know. Katie was snapping like an animal. She bit the nurse on the wrist and sent an angry fist flush into the face of an intern, bloodying his nose. New curses, kicks, and angry screams.

Hours later, after waking from a sedated sleep, Katie whispered: "I sort of remember . . . I hated everything, everything."

"Us, Katie? Mostly us?" Katie's father asked.

"No. Mostly me," she said, closing her eyes.

Later the staff psychiatrist visited Katie and reported to the bewildered parents: "Katie is a very upset young woman. She doesn't think much of herself. That's why she took the sleeping pills."

"But she's wonderful—always has been," the distraught Margaret Mattisson blurted out. "She must know it!"

The doctor remained calm. "She knew you thought so, and she tried to be, felt she *had* to be, what you thought she was. That's what she was telling us last night."

"Why didn't she tell it to us before? We always talked," the puzzled mother asked.

"She didn't want to disappoint you—didn't want anyone to think she wasn't as nice as they all thought she was. We all want to be loved, you know. She thought acting nice is what made people love her—even her parents. She doesn't think she is a person, so dying doesn't matter."

Katie's parents responded that they had loved her, and asked how it was possible that Katie could hate herself.

The doctor replied: "Love is not enough. You can't exist as the reflection of someone's love. You have to be your own person."

All the time that Katie presented herself as the ideal daughter and young lady there was inside her a seething resentment and self-contempt. Her parents had built a pedestal for her and she climbed up on it. For years she played the role because she thought it was the admission price for being loved.

At last—thanks perhaps to Katie's shattering and almost disastrous attempt to die—the parents understood and Katie recovered. The essential and most valuable thing she recovered, of course, was her self, her own individual, unique, and unrepeatable person.

Thank you, Margaret Mattisson, and thank you, Katie, for sharing your story. The lesson is so easy to lose, to forget. We must all be sure that those to whom we are committed in love know that there is no price tag, no admission price on our love. I have given you my love freely. It is my gift to you. There is no fine print in the contract, no hidden agenda. Love is the purest and simplest of gifts. Most people want to be very sure that their love is not taken for granted. Unconditional love says the very opposite: "Take me, and take my love for granted." In the words of the contemporary hymn: "All I ask of you is forever to remember me as loving you."

Giving and Receiving Love

When we talk about the kind of love with which we want to be loved, most of us would clearly and emphatically specify that it be unconditional. I don't want you to love me for what I can do for you or because I please your expectations. I want you to love me for better or worse, in sickness and in health, in good times and in bad, for richer or for poorer, with no strings attached. I can't sell out my person to buy your love.

However, when we are discussing the kind of love which we are willing to give, it is not so clear. Most of us want to be more tentative in case things don't work out. To give my word and to promise unconditional faithfulness to that word is more than a little frightening. We want to leave a back door open, an escape hatch. It is so much easier to be an unencumbered butterfly, flitting from flower to flower. It is so much harder to take the plunge into an unconditional commitment. It seems much less frightening to travel with a tent than to build a permanent home.

In Fear and Trembling: Commitment

What do we fear in the promise of unconditional love? For sure there are many uncertainties. I almost always think at weddings what a marvelous act of trust two people make in themselves and in each other when they promise that nothing will ever come between them with a power to separate them. As they make their vows, they certainly know something at least of what this will involve. There will be days when the well of warm feelings will run dry, when the decision of fidelity will be tested. There will be long and gray days when the rewards of loving will seem like distant memories or faint hopes. And still they will have the courage to say before all the

world: "As long as I shall live, I will be your man
. . . your woman." It is a real profession of belonging,
a life wager, a choice that will change two lives and
unite two persons forever in love.

When a couple exchanges rings on their wedding
day, I think of the symbolism. The circle of the ring
is symbolic of the endlessness of love. There are, of
course, other young people who express cynicism
about marriage, saying that it is "only a piece of
paper." I feel very sympathetic when I hear this,
because I presume that such people have never
experienced a committed and unconditional love. But
I also feel very sad because I see marriage as the only
public profession of unconditional love which we
have left in our society.

I do have a very real sympathy for the doubters.
As in so many other similar matters, experience
seems to lie at the heart of the matter. We tend to
generalize from our own experience. If I have never
had the experience of unconditional love—either as
a giver or receiver—I tend to doubt its existence. I
tend to disbelieve those who claim the experience.

*"Love is not enough. You can't exist
as the reflection of someone's love."*

On the other hand, if I have ever, even once, known the security of a love without conditions, I need no further explanations or proof.

The Haunting Fear

Perhaps the most disturbing of all fears is that my commitment of unconditional love will somehow be a denial or surrender of my self, a sad farewell to a sense of separate identity. I fear that I will have to give up my individual interests and personal tastes. In fact, if these fears were realized, there could be no relationship of love because relationship means two. Kahlil Gibran in his book *The Prophet* says that unconditional love should not be conceived as making two islands into one solid landmass. A love relationship, he suggests, should rather be like two islands that remain separate and distinct, but whose shores are washed by the shared waters of love. Rainer Maria Rilke says: "Love consists in this: that two solitudes protect and touch and greet each other." A person might possibly surrender his or her own identity to another out of lack of respect for self or out of the need for approval, but one can never do this in the name of true love.

More specifically, loving you does not mean that I cease to love myself. On the contrary, the idea that I cannot love you unless I love myself is universally accepted by psychologists. Those who do not love themselves are sad, plagued by a constant sense of emptiness which they are always trying to fill. Like a person with a toothache, they can think only of themselves and they are constantly in search of a dentist, someone to make them feel better. If I do not love myself, I can only *use* others; I cannot *love* them.

My loving you can never be an abdication of my own self. I could possibly give my life for you out of love, but I could never deny my identity as a person. I will try to be what you need me to be, to do what you need done, to say whatever you need to hear. At the same time I am committed to an honest and open relationship. As a part of my gift of love, I will always offer my thoughts, preferences, and all my feelings, even when I think they may be unpleasant or even hurtful to your feelings. If we are committed to total honesty and total openness, our relationship will never be a sticky one, marked by hidden agenda, repressed resentments, displaced emotions, acting out in adolescent ways what we do not have the courage to speak out. Unless we agree to honor honesty and openness, we will never be sure of each other. Our relationship will seem more like a charade than a real life drama.

I Promise You a Person

Finally, in my commitment of unconditional love I promise you a person, not a piece of putty. A "person" means that I have rights, as well as responsibilities. I have a right, for example, to express my own thoughts and feelings, to have my own preferences and the liberty to follow them. I also have an area of personal choice which is mine, and I must insist on keeping this area for myself. Making my own decisions and taking responsibility for them is an essential part of the human maturation process. Of course, I will never make decisions which involve both of us, but there are decisions that I must make for myself. These are some of the rights implied in being a person, and I intend to assert these rights and to insist that you respect them. Be ready to find in me a person you can bump into. Of course, you have a corresponding set of rights, and I will try to be very careful in respecting them. I will not only respect your rights, but I will expect you to exercise your own personhood in asserting these rights and in insisting on my respect for them.

And please have the courage to tell me at all times what you are thinking and feeling. I have no X-ray eyes to know your hidden thoughts or feelings. I cannot guess your preferences. You must tell me. Making assumptions is a dangerous game. Do not think you are loving me by playing chameleon or by twisting yourself into a pretzel shape trying to please me. If you do, I will probably tire of you or become bored with you. I will certainly feel unchallenged by you and by our relationship.

Lastly, I cannot ever let you use or manipulate me. We must love persons and use things. I am a person, not a thing. To let you use me would be no act of love, either for you or for myself. Please understand that I will never set myself up as your judge. I cannot now nor will I ever be able to read your intentions. I can know your intentions only by asking you. But I will never allow your temper tantrums or your tears to compromise my communication. If I feel suspicious of you, I will confront you with my feelings. If I feel hurt by something you have said or done, I will say "Ouch!" When you affirm or console or congratulate me, I will forever be visibly grateful to you. The me that shall be yours will be the unabridged and unedited version. In the words of the poet Richard Lovelace: "I could not love thee, dear, so much/Lov'd I not honor more."

I am an actor, not a reactor. This means that I must always decide how I am going to act. I cannot put this responsibility in your hands. I will try to combine as much tact and kindness as I can with my honesty and openness, but I can never allow myself to be manipulated into a compromise, either in conduct or in communication. My thoughts and my feelings are not for hire. I will not be used.

Whatever else love may ask of us, it does not ask us to be doormats or peace-at-any-price persons. The primary gift of love is the offering of one's most honest self through one's most honest self-disclosure.

CHAPTER FOUR

The dynamics of love

When I want to be free at all costs
I am already beginning to bind myself
When I pursue my own wishes
I throw myself in chains
I do what I don't want to do
I am at my own mercy

And when I finally consider myself free
Freedom becomes a burden
Because I must make decisions
Which I am unable to make
And my freedom turns into a new prison

I can only find freedom
In the ropes that bind me
To you

ULRICH SCHAFFER

The Three Stages of Love

In the process of loving there are three important stages or moments:

1. *Kindness:*
   a warm assurance that "I am on your side. I care about you."

2. *Encouragement:*
   a strong reassurance of your own strength and self-sufficiency.

3. *Challenge:*
   a loving but firm exhortation to action.

It has been said that loving is an art and this means that there are no scientific-type formulae that can be applied to guarantee successful results. One must take constant readings of the relational situation and try to judge what is needed, when to apply it, and how much of it to apply. Just as an artist-painter uses canvas and oils to achieve certain desired effects, so the artist-lover must try to sense when the need is for more kindness, more encouragement, or more challenge. It is never easy.

Kindness. Someone has wisely said that "people do not care how much you know until they know how much you care." I am sure that this is the foundation of love: a communicated caring about the happiness of the one loved and an affirmation or reassurance of that loved one's worth. To build a relationship on any other foundation is to build on sand. I have to know that you really want my happiness and my growth, that you really are "for me," or I won't open at all to your influence.

I must understand that I am a person to you, not just a thing. I must know that I am not simply a "case" to be treated, or a "problem" to be solved. And so, the first thing that love must do is communicate these three things: I truly care about you. I really want your happiness and I will do all I can to assure it. You are a uniquely valuable person.

Encouragement. For a long time in my own life, I would like to admit to you, I thought of love as doing acts of kindness for others. I even fell victim to the delusion that doing things for others which they could have and should have done for themselves was really love. If a person were painfully shy, I would leap into action, saving them from the distress involved in self-assertion. For the indecisive, I was a repository of answers. Every person who ever submitted a problem to me was immediately blessed with an instant solution. I never let others struggle long enough to win a victory for or over themselves.

Gradually the truth settled in on me. The settling in started when someone suggested to me: "Give a man a fish and he can eat for a day. Teach him to fish and he can eat for a lifetime." The application was obvious. Shy, indecisive, and struggling people may welcome or even invite us to provide for them. They may even say "I can't" when they really mean "I don't want to put out whatever is needed." They may try various forms of manipulation to hitchhike on the stability, decisiveness, or assertiveness of others. And we average persons are tempted. We are very vulnerable, in fact, to such manipulation. It is more immediately gratifying to say, "Of course, I will do it for you," or to offer the advice, "What you really need to do is this. . . ." The right response in such cases usually provides much less immediate gratification. "Oh, come on, you can do it. . . . I don't know what you should do. You have a good mind and you are capable of making decisions. What do you think you should do?"

When we cave in and allow others to be only persons-by-proxy, we train them to need us. They have to come back to us to get their deeds done and their problems solved. We develop clienteles of progressively weaker people in need of a "fix." We train them to be addicts in need of us. It is not at all loving.

One of the hardest-to-accept facts about true love is that it is liberating. Love offers a person *roots* (a sense of belonging) and *wings* (a sense of independence and freedom). What people really need is belief in themselves, confidence in their own ability to take on the problems and opportunities of life. This is what is meant by the second stage of love: encouragement. To en-courage means to put courage in. It instills into the recipient a new and fuller awareness of his or her own powers, strength, and self-sufficiency. Encouragement says: You can do it!

Challenge. The final stage of love is challenge. After conveying kindness ("I am for you!") and implanting courage ("You can do it!"), true love should then invite the beloved to "stretch," to grow beyond the old limitations, to attempt what was always considered too difficult, to break a self-destructive habit that has always been too overpowering, to rise above a fear, to give up a grudge, to open a repressed feeling, to confront a difficult situation, to offer a painful apology.

If encouragement makes the one loved aware of his or her strength, challenge is the loving push to actually use this strength: "Try. Stretch. Do it. If you succeed, I will be in the front row clapping my hands off. If you fail, I will be sitting right at your side. You won't be alone. Go ahead now. Give it your best shot. You can do it!"

Loving and "Growing Up"

Many nice, bland things can be said of love. For example, "Love divides one's burdens in half." An old monastic saying has it that "where there is love there is no labor." We sometimes roast the people we love, but we always have a toast for love: "If we only have love . . ." Love should indeed be toasted as the secret of a full and meaningful life, but it is no favor to love to romanticize it. T. S. Eliot once remarked that sometimes we "cannot stand too much reality." And Ionesco has made the observation that we are "forever trying to turn real life into literature."

The truth about love, I think, is that it is indeed a profound comfort, but it is also a monumental challenge. Love immediately challenges me to break the fixation I have with myself. It will drag me all the way from my infantile *id* to a complete self-donation to a cause or to a person in freely given love. Love demands that I learn how to focus my attention on the needs of those I love. It will ask me to become a sensitive listener. At times love will insist that I postpone my own gratifications to meet the needs of those I love. The kind of communication which is the lifeblood of love will require me to get in touch with my most sensitive feelings and my most buried thoughts, and to share these in the frightening act of self-disclosure. Love will make me vulnerable. It

It is no favor to love to romanticize it.

will open me to the honest reactions of others whom I have allowed to penetrate my defenses. If I have built protective walls around my vulnerable places, love will tear them down.

Love will teach me to give and to receive without pan-scales. Love transcends pan-scale justice. If love divides the burdens of life in half by sharing, it also doubles one's responsibilities. Two do not eat as cheaply as one, unless one of the two does not eat. It is also true that two cannot make decisions as quickly as one. Two are not as mobile as one, and so forth.

In other words, if you don't want to—

- break the fixation with self and give up your self-centeredness,
- learn how to care about and be sincerely dedicated to the satisfaction of another,
- become a sensitive listener, who hears what is said and some things that are not able to be said,
- postpone personal gratification to meet the needs of another,
- get in touch with your deepest feelings and most hidden thoughts,
- share your most vulnerable self as an act of love,
- get honest feedback from someone who really knows you through your own self-disclosure,

- give up your pan-scales and be prepared to give 100 percent,
- take on the added responsibilities for a "we,"
- work at the delicate art of dialogue and shared decision making,

. . . if you don't want these things, then obviously you don't want love. If you prefer to be an island, a recluse, a narcissist, preferring to live in a world that has a population of one, love would rip out of your hands everything that you hold dear and clutch tightly.

And yet, it seems obvious to me, as I feel sure it will seem to you, that these very challenges of a true love relationship, which assault our self-centeredness, are in fact the bridge to human maturity and ultimate human fulfillment. Viktor Frankl writes:

> A thought transfixed me: for the first time in my life I saw the truth as it is set into song by so many poets, proclaimed as the final wisdom by so many thinkers. The truth— that love is the ultimate and the highest goal to which man can aspire. Then I grasped the meaning of the greatest secret that human poetry and human thought and belief have to impart: *the salvation of man is through love and in love.*
>
> **Man's Search for Meaning**

Another great psychiatrist, Dr. Karl Menninger, liked to repeat: "Love cures. It cures those who give it and it cures those who receive it." Even the great doctors, with whom we had previous occasion to disagree, are unanimous in the praise of love and love relationships as the chief source of human maturation. When Sigmund Freud was asked for a definition of mental and emotional health, he said: "It is the capacity to work and to love." Likewise, Alfred Adler said that "all human failures are the result of a lack of love." More and more psychologists are coming to esteem the capacity for intimacy. People with low capacities for love relationships are ten times more likely to be labeled psychiatrically ill. The command of Jesus that we love one another seems to be a human imperative rather than an option. The experimental evidence for the crippling effects of a loveless life is found in the office of every psychiatrist, filled with children and adults who have no awareness of their own worth, no sense of identity, who are filled with hatred and fear and tortured by anxieties. Love is costly, but the alternatives are deadly.

Love demands that I learn how to focus my attention on the needs of those I love.

The Challenges
and the Comforts

Michael Novak has written of marriage and family in words I would like to share with you. What he says in the following lengthy excerpt, originally published in *Harper's Magazine,* is applicable, I think, to any true commitment of love:

> In our society, of course, there is no need to become an adult. One may remain—one is daily exhorted to remain—a child forever. In such a life, the central aim is self-fulfillment. Marriage is merely an alliance, entailing as minimal an abridgment of inner privacy as one partner may allow. Children are not a welcome responsibility, for to have children is, plainly, to cease being a child oneself. One tries instead to live as the angels were once believed to live—soaring, free, unencumbered.
>
> People say of marriage that it is boring, when what they mean is that it terrifies them: too many and too deep are its searing revelations, its angers, its rages, its hates, and its loves. They say of marriage that it is deadening, when what they mean is that it drives us beyond adolescent fantasies and romantic dreams. They say of children that

they are piranhas, brats, snots, when what
they mean is that the importance of parents
with respect to the future of their children is
now known with greater clarity and exacti-
tude than ever before.

Being married and having children has
impressed on my mind certain lessons, and
most of what I am forced to learn about
myself is not pleasant. The quantity of sheer
impenetrable selfishness in the human breast
(in *my* breast) is a never-failing source of
wonderment. I do not want to be disturbed,
challenged, troubled. Huge regions of myself
belong only to me. Seeing myself through the
unblinking eyes of an intelligent, honest
spouse is humiliating. Trying to act fairly to
children, each of whom is temperamentally
different from myself and from each other, is.
baffling. My family bonds hold me back from
many opportunities. And yet these bonds are,
I know, my liberation. They force me to be a
different sort of human being in a way I want
and need.

MICHAEL NOVAK,
"The Family Out of Favor"

Novak goes on to say that it would be a lie to write
only of the difficulties and not of the beauty of love.
In fact, I think, weathering the storms of the love
process is the only way to find the rainbows of life.

The comforts that one finds on the "less-traveled road" of love are found nowhere else. Life has a much deeper meaning when I truly love another. The loneliness of a world that has a population of one is filled by a new and warm presence when love enters a life. The self-alienation of the old person who could not interact intimately is replaced in the person renewed by love by a sense of self and of self-worth. It is what we call today a sense of "identity." It has become a truism that we can know and love only as much of ourselves as we are willing to share with another in love. The aimless wandering of the loveless person finds in love a sense of belonging and a place called home.

Going out to another in love means risk—the risks of self-disclosure, rejection, misunderstanding. It means grief, too, from the temporary separations, psychological or physical, to the final separation of death. Whoever insists on personal security and

The crippling effects of a loveless life
are found in the office of every psychiatrist,
filled with children and adults
who have no awareness of their own worth,
no sense of identity.

safety as the nonnegotiable conditions of life will not
be willing to pay love's price or find love's enrich-
ments. Whoever shuts himself or herself up in the
cocoon of self-protective defenses, keeping others
always at a safe distance and holding on tightly to
personal possessions and privacy, will find the price
of love far too high and will remain forever a prisoner
of fear. Erich Fromm writes:

> To be loved, and to love, need courage, the
> courage to judge certain values as of ultimate
> concern—and to take the jump and stake
> everything on these values.
>
> **The Art of Loving**

CHAPTER FIVE

The God of love

Some day,
after we have mastered the winds,
the waves, the tides and gravity,
we will harness for God
the energies of love
and then for the second time
in the history of the world
man will have discovered fire.
PIERRE TEILHARD DE CHARDIN, S.J.

In the Old Testament God reveals himself to the
People of Israel as a God of unconditional love. His
gift of himself in the choice and creation of "my
People" is totally unsolicited, undeserved, and unmerited. In the seventh chapter of Deuteronomy it
is very clear that God's love for his People was not
based on anything they were or had. The Hebrew
word used to describe this kind of covenanted and
unconditional love is *hesed*. It can be translated as
"loving kindness," but *hesed* clearly implies that this
love is an unmerited gift and an irrevocable commitment. God decides, God chooses, God offers his gift
of love. He is by his own free act forever committed
to his People. The prophet Hosea uses the image of
God taking a bride: "And I will betroth you to me
forever" (2:19–20). Through the prophet Isaiah, God
says: "Even if a mother should forget the child of her
womb, I will never forget you" (49:15).

The unconditionality of God's love for his People
is a constant refrain in the Old Testament. God has
promised and God will always be faithful to his
promise. Jeremiah writes of God's constant willing-
ness to forgive: "With an eternal love I have loved
you. Therefore, in loving-kindness I draw you to
myself" (31:3). It is a striking anticipation of Jesus'
parable of the prodigal son: "And while he was still
a long distance away, his father saw him coming,
and was filled with loving pity and ran and embraced
him and kissed him" (Luke 15:20).

Jesus: God's Word of Love

Saint Paul calls Jesus the "visible image of our invisible God" (Colossians 1:15). To his contemporaries Jesus was a rabbi, and by the tradition of the times should have spent his time deciding cases of the law. But Jesus kept talking about love, and his contemporaries found this very irritating. They encouraged him to be a legal interpreter; they kept presenting to him cases to be adjudged. "Good Master [Rabbi], this man's oxen have fallen into a ditch on the Sabbath, and we want to know if he can pull them out. . . . Good Master, are we obliged to pay taxes to Rome? . . . Good Master, we have caught this woman in the sin of adultery. Now we have a law that says she should be stoned to death. . . . Good Master, what do you say? . . . Good Master. . . ?"

And Jesus kept telling them that this kind of microscopic attention to the letter of the law kills the spirit of love. "Oh, don't worry," he assured them, "I have not come to destroy the law but to fulfill it, to subsume, to elevate the whole law into one great commandment: love! You can self-righteously keep the law in every detail without loving, but you can't truly love without keeping the law. If you really love, you will keep the law: you won't steal or lie or kill, not if you really love." This was the summary response of Jesus, if not his exact words.

He was telling them something like this: "Don't deal with God legalistically. That's the way you deal with someone you fear. You worry about the punishments of an authority whom you fear, so you do everything he demands and then you feel safe. Then you can say, 'I have done everything you demanded. You cannot punish me now!' This is not really a 'Yes!' of love to either God or neighbor. It is really a small and frightened person saying an emphatic 'No!' to personal insecurity. God is not calling you to this fearful submission, but rather to love him with your whole mind and heart and soul and your neighbor as yourself!"

But they didn't understand. And it really wouldn't have been so bad, they whispered to each other, if only he weren't so soft on sinners. He kept associating with tax collectors and prostitutes. He kept eating and drinking with socially, if not totally, disreputable people.

He thought of himself as some kind of "Good Shepherd in love with and in search of straying sheep." He said he was the "Divine Physician" who did not come for the healthy and wealthy but for the poor, the sick, and the needy. He once scandalized the whole self-righteous set when he allowed a prostitute to cry all over his feet and then to dry them with her bleached hair at the house of Simon the Pharisee. The worst part was that he praised her for her . . . get this, love! He said that wherever the story of his life was told, down through the centuries and out to the ends of the earth, the story of that woman and what she did for him would also be told. It was just too much!

The Confrontation and the Parable

So the doubters confronted Jesus one day, and pressed the question they knew he couldn't safely answer. They stood around him like an iron horseshoe of hostility. It was his last chance. If he didn't conform or at least compromise now, then it would be better that one man should die than that the whole nation (and all its laws) should perish. They knew it. He knew it.

They asked: "What does God think of a sinner?"

So he told the story of unconditional love. We call it the parable of the prodigal son. It is the story of a kind and loving father and his two sons. The younger son feels that he has outgrown his father, and wants no part of his father's life-style or home. He lays claim to his inheritance and leaves his father without even looking back over his shoulder. The father allows his son this liberty of choice, but he waits on the front porch of the little farmhouse every night, hoping and watching the road from the city. Others coming back from the city deliver shattering reports.

"Hey Mister, you ought to be declared 'Father of the Year' for siring that fuzzbrain son of yours. You should see your little blue-eyed boy—seducing every available and vulnerable woman, when he isn't too drunk or involved in some other stupidity."

But the father continues to wait there every night until darkness settles over the land. When it is dark, he goes inside and goes to bed, saying a tearful prayer for his boy, his lost but always dear son.

Then one night, there on the front porch, his heart nearly explodes with excitement. He sees a figure coming down the road. He can tell . . . it is his son! His son is coming home. The father runs down the road, his heart pounding and his eyes filling with tears, the tears of relief. All Scripture scholars say that no father in that time and culture would have run to his son. It would have seemed totally strange and out of place. It could have happened only to someone whose explosion of joy overcame all sense of time and place and social custom.

The father hugs his boy tightly, huge racking sobs of joy shaking his body. Warm tears roll down his cheeks. The boy is saying something about not being worthy to come home as a son, and asking only to hire on as a field worker. The father hears nothing of this. His heart is saying: "I don't care where you've been or what you've done. All I really care about is that you are home . . . you're home!" The father swallows hard, swallows the warm tears gathered in his throat, and calls for rings and robes and music makers. He orders the fatted calf killed and roasted over an open fire. This is to be a party to end all parties. "My boy is home!" When the older son comes in from the fields to discover the party in full swing, he does not understand. He is angry: "You never gave a party for me and my friends."

"Oh Son," the father says, "I do understand. I love you so much. And I am very grateful for your faithfulness. You have stayed here with me. Everything I have is yours. Anytime you want a party for yourself and your friends, everything I have will be at your disposal. But there is something I must ask you to understand. Would you please try to understand what goes on in the heart of a father when his lost child comes home?"

The question hung there in the emotionally charged atmosphere: "Would you please try to understand what goes on in the heart of a father when his lost child comes home?" Jesus looked squarely around the horseshoe of hostile faces and said: "This is what God thinks of a sinner!"

The question was answered. He would offer his life in the end for that answer. But he would die as he had lived, unconditionally loving.

He would say "Shalom! Be at peace. I understand" to the frightened Apostles who had left him to die alone. He would die praying for the very people who had crucified him: "Father, forgive them, for they do not know what they are doing." In the end he would die between two thieves. It was somehow fitting that he who spent his life caring for and searching out the rejected should die between two thieves. One of the thieves looked at the plaque over the head of Jesus, indicating the crime for which he was dying. It read: "This is Jesus of Nazareth, the King of the Jews." The thief looked with plaintive eyes into the eyes of Jesus: "I know nothing about your kingdom, but when you come into your kingdom, would you remember me?"

These were the last words that Jesus would speak to any person before his death. He said: "This day you will be with me in paradise."

Under every crucifix, depicting the Lord with his heart opened and his hands stretched out as if to embrace all the weak and the wounded of this world, there should be a caption reading:

"This is what I mean when I say I love you!"

But he would die as he had lived, unconditionally loving.

If the parable of the prodigal son is the story of unconditional love, Jesus on his cross is the portrait of such love. Like love itself the person of Jesus is both a comfort and a challenge. The comfort is more profound than anything we have ever experienced. The "Shalom! Be at peace. I understand" is always held out to us, and especially at those times when we feel like old Peter the rock and sometimes sandpile: "Depart from me, Lord," Peter moaned, "for I am a sinful man!" But, of course, unconditional love doesn't ever depart. Jesus asked Peter, as he asks us, only this: "Do you love me?" He does not ask about our weakness but only about our love.

The challenge is: "Love one another as I have loved you!"

Love: God's Port of Entry

God's love for each of us is just as unsolicited, unmerited, and unconditional as was his love for the People of Israel. Jesus is the Word of this love, uttered into the world. God comes to us in him, wanting to share, to communicate his goodness, joy, and love. He wants to love us into the fullness of life.

On the human level all of us have at some time experienced this kind of inner urge and insistence to share something good: good news, a good joke, a good tip. At an even deeper level it is the inner urge of artists to share with others a vision of beauty, the music that they have heard inside themselves. At the deepest human level it is the desire of procreation: when two people love each other very much, they want to share their love and their lives with a new life, fashioned by God from their own flesh and blood. It is something like this with God. The impetus of God's love comes from within himself, to share with us his life and love. It is a free gift, freely given, not earned or deserved or claimed by any right of ours. It is a beautiful, eternal gift, held out to us in the hands of love. It is an unconditional covenant.

All we have to do is say "Yes!" All we have to do is open ourselves to receive this pearl of great price, this love that will transform us and every moment of our lives. The key word is openness.

The little child who is inside me wishes that openness were simple. The fact is that the big "Yes!" of openness has many other little "yeses" inside it. Some of them will be very costly. Some will call for great courage. Some will be uttered in darkness.

Saying "Yes!" to God's gift of love and life primarily and above all means *choosing love as a life principle*. The Apostle John, for whom Jesus seemed to have a special love, says in his First Epistle:

> We know how much God loves us because we have felt his love and because we believe him when he tells us that he loves us dearly.

God is love, and anyone who lives in love is
living with God and God is living in him.

1 John 4:16

Saying "Yes!" to God is not a simple matter
because making our lives into lives of love is not a
simple or easy thing. To choose love as a life principle
means that my basic mind-set or question must be:
What is the loving thing to be, to do, to say? My
consistent response to each of life's events, to each
person who enters and touches my life, to each
demand on my time and nerves and heart, must
somehow be transformed into an act of love.
However, in the last analysis, it is this "Yes!" that
opens me to God. Choosing love as a life principle
widens the chalice of my soul, so that God can pour
into me his gifts and graces and powers.

Tommy

About fifteen years ago, I stood watching my
university students file into the classroom for our
first session in the Theology of Faith. That was the
day I first saw Tommy. My eyes and my mind both
blinked. He was combing his long flaxen hair, which
hung six inches below his shoulders. It was the first
time I had ever seen a boy with hair that long. I guess
it was just coming into fashion then. I know in my
mind that it isn't what's on your head but in it that
counts, but on that day I was unprepared and my

emotions flipped. I immediately filed Tommy under "S" for strange . . . very strange.

Tommy turned out to be the "atheist in residence" in my Theology of Faith course. He constantly objected to, smirked at, or whined about the possibility of an unconditionally loving Father-God. We lived with each other in relative peace for one semester, although I admit he was for me at times a serious pain in the back pew. When he came up at the end of the course to turn in his final exam, he asked in a slightly cynical tone: "Do you think I'll ever find God?" I decided instantly on a little shock therapy. "No!" I said very emphatically. "Oh," he responded, "I thought that was the product you were pushing." I let him get five steps from the classroom door and then called out: "Tommy! I don't think you'll ever find him, but I am absolutely certain that he will find you!" He shrugged a little and left my class and my life (temporarily). I felt slightly disappointed at the thought that he had missed my clever line: "He will find you!" At least I thought it was clever.

Later I heard that Tom was graduated and I was duly grateful. Then a sad report. I heard that Tommy had terminal cancer. Before I could search him out, he came to see me. His body was badly wasted, and the long hair had all fallen out as a result of chemotherapy. But his eyes were bright and his voice was firm, for the first time, I think. "Tommy, I've thought about you so often. I hear you are sick!" I blurted out.

"Oh, yes, very sick. I have cancer in both lungs. It's a matter of weeks."

"Can you talk about it, Tom?"

"Sure, what would you like to know?"

"What's it like to be only twenty-four and dying?"

"Well, it could be worse."

"Like what?"

"Well, like being fifty and having no values or ideals, like being fifty and thinking that booze, seducing women, and making money are the real 'biggies' in life."

I began to look through my mental file cabinet under "S" where I had filed Tom as strange. (I swear that everybody I try to reject by classification God sends back into my life to educate me.)

"But what I really came to see you about," Tom said, "is something you said to me on the last day of class." (He remembered!)

He continued, "I asked you if you thought I would ever find God and you said, 'No!' which surprised me. Then you said, 'But he will find you.' I thought about that a lot, even though my search for God was hardly intense at that time. (My "clever" line. He thought about that a lot!)

"But when the doctors removed a lump from my groin and told me that it was malignant, then I got serious about locating God. And when the malignancy spread into my vital organs, I really began banging bloody fists against the bronze doors of heaven. But God did not come out. In fact, nothing happened. Did you ever try anything for a long time with great effort and with no success? You get psychologically glutted, fed up with trying. And then you quit. Well, one day I woke up, and instead of throwing a few more futile appeals over that high brick wall to a God who may be or may not be there, I just quit. I decided that I didn't really care . . . about God, about an afterlife, or anything like that.

"I decided to spend what time I had left doing something more profitable. I thought about you and your class and I remembered something else you had said: 'The essential sadness is to go through life without loving. But it would be almost equally sad to go through life and leave this world without ever telling those you loved that you had loved them.'

"So I began with the hardest one: my dad. He was reading a newspaper when I approached him."

"Dad . . ."

"Yes, what?" he asked without lowering the newspaper.

"Dad, I would like to talk with you."

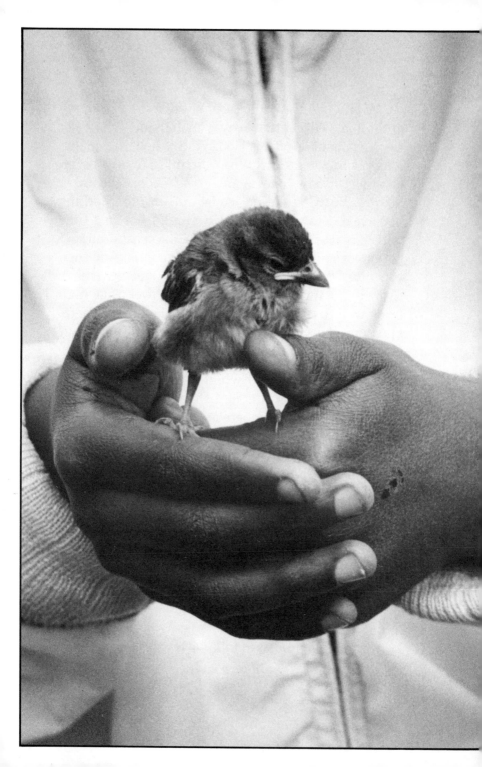

"Well, talk."

"I mean . . . It's really important."

The newspaper came down three slow inches. "What is it?"

"Dad, I love you. I just wanted you to know that."

Tom smiled at me and said with obvious satisfaction, as though he felt a warm and secret joy flowing inside of him: "The newspaper fluttered to the floor. Then my father did two things I could never remember him ever doing before. He cried and he hugged me. And we talked all night, even though he had to go to work the next morning. It felt so good to be close to my father, to see his tears, to feel his hug, to hear him say that he loved me.

"It was easier with my mother and little brother. They cried with me, too, and we hugged each other, and started saying real nice things to each other. We shared the things we had been keeping secret for so many years. I was only sorry about one thing: that I had waited so long. Here I was, in the shadow

The big "Yes!" of openness has many other little "yeses" inside it.

of death, and I was just beginning to open up to all the people I had actually been close to.

"Then, one day I turned around and God was there. He didn't come to me when I pleaded with him. I guess I was like an animal trainer holding out a hoop, 'C'mon, jump through. C'mon, I'll give you three days . . . three weeks.' Apparently God does things in his own way and at his own hour.

"But the important thing is that he was there. He found me. You were right. He found me even after I stopped looking for him."

"Tommy," I practically gasped, "I think you are saying something very important and much more universal than you realize. To me, at least, you are saying that the surest way to find God is not to make him a private possession, a problem solver, or an instant consolation in time of need, but rather by opening to love. You know, Saint John said that. He said 'God is love, and anyone who lives in love is living with God and God is living in him.'

"Tom, could I ask you a favor? You know, when I had you in class you were a real pain. But (laughingly) you can make it all up to me now. Would you come into my present Theology of Faith course and tell them what you have just told me? If I told them the same thing, it wouldn't be half as effective as if you were to tell them."

"Oooh . . . I was ready for you, but I don't know if I'm ready for your class."

"Tom, think about it. If and when you are ready, give me a call."

In a few days Tommy called, said he was ready for the class, that he wanted to do that for God and for me. So we scheduled a date. However, he never made it. He had another appointment, far more important than the one with me and my class. Of course, his life was not really ended by his death, only changed. He made the great step from faith into vision. He found a life far more beautiful than the human eye has ever seen or the human ear has ever heard or the human mind has ever imagined.

Before he died, we talked one last time. "I'm not going to make it to your class," he said.

"I know, Tom."

"Will you tell them for me? Will you . . . tell the whole world for me?"

"I will, Tom. I'll tell them. I'll do my best."

So, to all of you who have been kind enough to hear this simple statement about love, thank you for listening. And to you, Tom, somewhere in the sunlit, verdant hills of heaven:

"I told them, Tommy . . . as best I could."

Acknowledgments

Continued from page ii

Richard and Clara Winston. Copyright © 1963. Reprinted by permission of Pantheon Books, a Division of Random House, Inc.

Excerpt from G. Marian Kinget, *On Being Human*. Copyright © 1975. Reprinted by permission of Harcourt Brace Jovanovich, Inc.

The text of Colossians 3:14, John 5:2-9, I John 4:16, Luke 4:1-12, and Luke 15:20 are taken from *The Living Bible,* copyright © 1971 by Tyndale House Publishers, Wheaton, Ill. Used by permission.

Poem by Archibald MacLeish. Reprinted by permission of Houghton Mifflin Company. All rights reserved.

Excerpts from Margaret Mattison, "Love Is Not Enough." Adapted with permission from the February 1976 *Reader's Digest.* Copyright © 1976 by The Reader's Digest Association, Inc.

Excerpt from Michael Novak, "The Family Out of Favor." Copyright © 1976 by *Harper's Magazine.* All rights reserved. Excerpted from the April 1976 issue by special permission.

Frederick S. Perls, "Gestalt Prayer" on page 63. © Real People Press 1969. All rights reserved.

Specified excerpt from pages 84–85 from *The Bell Jar* by Sylvia Plath. Copyright © 1971 by Harper & Row, Publishers, Inc. Reprinted by permission of Harper & Row, Publishers, Inc., and Faber and Faber Ltd.

Poem on page 21 of *Searching for You* by Ulrich Schaffer. Copyright © 1978 by Ulrich Schaffer. Reprinted by permission of Harper & Row, Publishers, Inc.

Excerpt from Antoine de Saint-Exupéry, *The Little Prince,* translated by Katherine Woods. Copyright 1943. Reprinted by permission of Harcourt Brace Jovanovich, Inc., and William Heinemann, London.

Adapted excerpt from Pierre Teilhard de Chardin, S.J., "The Future of Chastity." Reprinted by permission of Georges Borchardt, Inc.

Walter Tubbs, "Beyond Perls," from *Journal of Humanistic Psychology,* 12 (Fall 1972), p. 5. Reprinted by permission of *Journal of Humanistic Psychology.*